我的目標是：生命眞的有意義

My Goal Is：Life Is Really Meaningful.

（中英雙語版）
(Chinese-English Bilingual Edition)

決長
Jue Chang

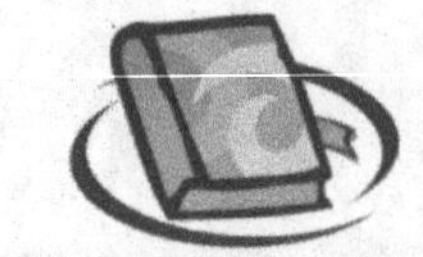

目錄

生命的意義與筆者的目標 ⋯⋯⋯⋯⋯⋯⋯⋯⋯⋯⋯⋯⋯⋯ 35

 我的目標是：生命真的有意義

Tables

The Meaning of Life and the Author's Goal.......80

我的目標是：生命真的有意義

序

　　筆者的故鄉是台灣，以前台灣信仰著傳統價值，台灣信仰著聖人的話，但聖人解答生命的意義了嗎？有人說生命有意義，有人說生命沒有意義，聖人沒有拿出證明。

　　筆者解答了這個人類歷史上最難的問題，只要準備實驗組跟對照組，可以證明人活著有應該做的事，所有人都應該思考、豐富心靈，生命的意義是「多元」。

　　筆者的目標是告訴大家：生命真的有意義。

　　「生命真的有意義，生命的意義是多元」，當筆者跟台灣人分享這個答案的時候，台灣舉辦了同性婚姻法的公投，但生命有意義了嗎？台灣人還是矛盾地說：善沒有標準答案。台灣人一邊喊著多元，一邊說同性婚姻法不一定是對的。

　　筆者說：生命「真的」有意義。

　　但台灣說：同性婚姻法不一定是對的。

　　當筆者跟台灣分享「多元」這個答案的時候，台灣的總統一邊到寺廟向傳統價值下跪，一邊喊著：「台灣價值是多元。」

　　台灣的總統、教育部長他們的「多元」不是完整的答案，為什麼多元是對的？為什麼傳統價值錯了？證明方法、尋找答案的過程、誰找到的？「以前沒答案，現在找到了」的這個宣稱呢？台灣找到方向了嗎？

　　台灣以前信仰傳統價值，

　　台灣現在喊著多元，

　　但台灣的多元是「真的」嗎？

所以本書的內容包含了這四個題目：

「同性婚姻法與生命的意義」、

「生命的意義與傳統價值」、

「生命的意義與完整的答案」、

「生命的意義與筆者的目標」。

筆者想要告訴大家：

生命「真的」有意義。

決長

2024、06、21

同性婚姻法與生命的意義

壹、前言。

　　筆者的故鄉是台灣，台灣已經通過同性婚姻法了，在亞洲，這是一件了不起的事，那接下來呢？台灣還要舉辦同志遊行嗎？要的，我們還要繼續深耕文化與觀念。

　　「人類淫亂而墮落，現在連同性都能結婚了，人類更加淫亂更加墮落了。」

　　有人這麼說。

　　「同性婚姻法是人權的進步。」

　　有人這麼說。

　　誰是對的呢？

　　理由呢？

　　人生有標準答案嗎？

　　本篇文章將說明：

　　一、同性婚姻法的理由。

　　二、舊觀念。

　　三、怎麼證明？

　　四、未來的方向。

　　人生沒有標準答案，同性婚姻法也許是進步？也許是墮落？是嗎？

　　本篇文章將說明：人生有標準答案，生命的意義是「多元」。

貳、同性婚姻法的理由。

同性婚姻法得來不易，

是很多人充滿勇氣地去衝撞舊觀念，

所以台灣才有同性婚姻法，

因為同性婚姻法得來不易，

所以，小朋友們，我們要支持多元。

學者們這樣教導下一代。

真是奇怪啊！

因為挺同團體很辛苦，所以我們要支持同性婚姻法，那反同團體就不辛苦嗎？

「因為得來不易，所以每個人都應該支持」這是一句完全沒有邏輯的話。

台灣的教育部喊著「多元價值」，但價值是沒有對與錯的，價值是沒有根據的，真是奇怪，大聲喊著價值，卻沒有說明同性婚姻的理由。在這個小節，筆者將說明同性婚姻的理由。

同性婚姻的理由是什麼呢？

是「多元價值」嗎？

不，同性婚姻不是虛幻的價值。

同性婚姻的理由是什麼呢？

答案是很單純的，

因為同志們就是相愛，

他們就是單純地想在一起，

所以他們希望能結婚、得到親友的祝福。

「相愛的人能在一起」

這就是同性婚姻的理由。

　我的目標是：生命真的有意義

同性婚姻的理由是什麼呢？

同志們認為「愛最大」。

而再仔細追究的話，

同性婚姻的理由是同志們的「我認為」。

參、舊觀念。

「同性婚姻法得來不易，

是很多人充滿勇氣地去衝撞舊觀念。」

那麼，舊觀念是什麼呢？

每年的十二月二十五日，地球上有許多人慶祝耶穌的生日，救主降生，處女生子，終生都是處女的聖母瑪利亞生下了耶穌，性行為是不好的，耶穌不是父母發生性行為之後生下的，創世紀中有亞當和夏娃的故事，人類因為吃了禁果被趕出伊甸園，啟示錄中有帶來災禍的大淫婦，

生命的意義是聽神的話，聖經教人守貞，情慾是觸怒上帝的罪業。

佛陀說生命的意義是回西方極樂世界，情感、慾望、享受、美女、美食、音樂都是蒙蔽心靈的塵埃，人們應該六根清淨、觀照本心，佛家也教人守貞，淫亂是觸犯戒律的罪，如果淫亂了，會墮入輪迴，靈魂會受到永遠的痛苦。

孔子說：君王要有君王的樣子，臣子要有臣子的樣子，父親要有父親的樣子，子女要有子女的樣子。

生命的意義是忠孝，我們要聽國王與父母的話，然後對國家做出貢獻，而女人應該忠於男人，遵守三從四德，在家從父、出嫁從

夫、夫死從子。

孔子說：我們要當君子，不要當禽獸，「禮」是國家的根本。基於「禮」，人們應該守貞，國家會為終身守貞不改嫁的女人立紀念碑，如果失去「禮」，國家將在淫亂與墮落中滅亡。

在舊觀念中，當青少年說長大後要當職業電競選手，有孔子思想的父母會反對，因為玩耍是對國家沒有貢獻的事。

當青少年說長大後要當搖滾樂手，有佛陀思想的父母會反對，因為搖滾樂會蒙蔽心靈。

當修女想要穿美麗的衣服，神父會反對，因為美麗的衣服是撒旦的誘惑。

個人興趣、玩耍、音樂、衣服都受到打壓了，那自由戀愛呢？宗教並不希望青少年談戀愛，也許青少年們認為談戀愛沒什麼大不了的，但父母非常擔心，不是擔心性病、懷孕，而是擔心如果靈魂染罪了，靈魂會受到永遠的刑罰，也擔心世界末日、大災難。

很多人都搞錯了，認為宗教反對同性婚姻，不，就算是異性的青少年談戀愛，宗教也是感到擔心的。

愛就該在一起，是嗎？

不，人應該克制自己的慾望，情慾與墮落會讓人類滅亡。

肆、疑惑與反抗。

生命的意義是回天堂，

當青少年談戀愛，愛上異性或同性，

父母會感到擔心，而同性戀也許會被強迫治療矯正。

愛就該在一起，是嗎？

　　很多同性戀們也感到疑惑，心中的愛與腦中的道德衝突著，該順從道德，當父母與耶穌喜愛的好孩子，還是該順從心中的愛呢？同性戀們自責、感到矛盾、無助、感到罪惡、希望被諒解、他們經歷了很長的無聲時光，躲藏著，不能攤在陽光下，他們自己都感到疑惑與罪惡，他們無法說出自己的主張。

　　當同性戀們累積力量，說出主張時，

　　他們說了和民主先烈一樣的話：

　　「自由」，

　　民主先烈向君王爭取自由，

　　而同性戀們沿用了民主先烈的答案，

　　我們是自由的，和相愛的人在一起是我們的自由，請不要干涉我們的自由。

　　歐洲、美國的同性戀喊著：

　　「善與惡不是二元對立的」，

　　善與惡沒有標準答案，人生沒有標準答案，請不要把道德強加於我們。

　　基於「自由」，基於「在一起是戀人的自由」，所以有些地方通過了同性婚姻法。

伍、自由的缺點。

　　基於自由，戀人們有結婚的自由，

　　但同性婚姻法是合於道德的嗎？

　　不知道，同性的戀人們只是想要在一起，

　　他們並沒有要挑戰耶穌。

　　同性婚姻法是墮落？

同性婚姻法是進步？

不知道，生命沒有標準答案。

我們應該教導下一代傳統價值？

我們應該教導下一代多元價值？

不知道，價值是主觀沒根據的，

未來是未知的，

老師們不確定什麼對下一代有益，

沒有人找到一定是對的事，

沒有人找到在未來還會是對的事，

人類找到未來的方向了嗎？

沒有，宗教說生命的意義是回天堂，

而哲學家說生命的意義沒有標準答案。

同志大遊行是一個呼口號的活動，

舊觀念是什麼？

舊觀念為什麼是錯的？

為什麼同性婚姻法代表著進步？

他們沒有回答這問題，

他們只會呼口號。

陸、筆者的答案。

生命的意義是人類歷史上最難的題目，未來是未知的，沒有人能指出未來的方向。

而筆者解答了這問題，筆者準備了實驗的方法：

　　只要準備維護環境的實驗組和不維護環境的對照組，可以證明人類必須維護環境，這是人類必須持續做的事。

　　只要停水、停電，可以證明人們必須關心故鄉，這是人類必須持續做的事。

　　只要準備實驗組和對照組，對照組的農夫、商店正常工作，實驗組的農夫、商店罷工，可以證明人們必須合作，人們必須合作一起吃飯。

　　只要準備一個空的房間和一個有娛樂有手機的房間，可以證明人有情感的需求，人類必須思考、必須豐富心靈，人類需要愛與歡笑。

　　只要準備你喜歡的食物和一百個志願者，觀察是否所有志願者都喜歡這食物，可以證明人有相同點，也有相異點，而這也是一個相同點，所有人都必須思考，所有人都必須認識自己的相異點。

　　這些都是人類必須持續做的事，是未來的方向，是生命的意義的答案。

　　筆者挑戰了耶穌、佛陀、孔子，

　　儒家說生命的意義是忠誠，而女人要忠於男人。孔子錯了，忠誠錯了，思考才是對的。

　　聖經說生命的意義是守貞回伊甸園，

　　聖經錯了，地球是人類唯一的家。

　　佛陀說情感、慾望是蒙蔽心靈的灰塵，

　　佛陀錯了，人類需要愛與歡笑。

　　生命的意義是多元，思考、填入愛與歡笑、豐富心靈、增加欣賞美的角度，這是人類要持續做的事，這是未來的方向。

柒、台灣的方向。

台灣曾經舉行同性婚姻法的公投，而同性戀們喊著「多元」，善與惡不是二元對立的，人生沒有標準答案，所以我們要多元。真是矛盾，善與惡沒有標準答案，所以你可以投贊成、你也可以投反對，善與惡沒有標準答案，也許我們應該通過同性婚姻法，也許我們應該為了保護青少年而禁止同性戀，善與惡沒有標準答案無法推論出台灣應該走向多元。

而當筆者說：「我解答生命的意義了，生命的意義是多元。」

台灣嘲笑著筆者，「笑死人了，生命的意義不會有答案啦。」然後他們說台灣有方向了，台灣的未來要走向多元。

台灣價值突然從抗中保台變成多元共好了。

同性戀們沒有挑戰耶穌，沒有解答未來的方向，台灣的方向不是天上掉下來的，筆者證明了台灣應該走向多元。

捌、結論。

台灣已經通過同性婚姻法了，

下一步是教育。

同性婚姻法是一個突破，是一個進步。

那麼舊的觀念是什麼？

舊的觀念為什麼是錯的？

多元的理由是什麼？怎麼證明？

為什麼多元不是墮落？

為什麼多元是進步？

請大聲說出來吧！

　我的目標是：生命真的有意義

未來有方向了，

決長解答了生命的意義，

生命的意義就是「多元」。

生命的意義與傳統價值

壹、前言。

筆者的故鄉是台灣，

台灣以前是威權的，

台灣現在走向民主，

學者和政治人物喊著：

「我們要改掉威權，

我們要走向進步的普世價值。」

真是奇怪，

普世價值是普世的嗎？

台灣有許多宗教，當選舉時，

總統會參拜每一間廟，

千年前的聖人真偉大，

老祖宗的智慧真偉大，

總統跪拜著，

真是奇怪，

千年前的智慧真偉大，

而我們要走向進步的普世價值。

這是一個矛盾。

本篇文章將說明：

一、傳統價值。

二、價值的衝突。

三、普世價值。

四、筆者的答案。

「人類應該怎麼活？

我們應該走向怎樣的未來？」

這問題有答案了嗎？

舊的答案是什麼？

新的觀念是什麼？

有什麼衝突？

本篇文章將說明傳統價值與觀念的衝突。

貳、傳統價值。

「人類應該怎麼活？」

這不是一個生而知之的問題，

算了，不用想太多，

答案就是「弱肉強食」，

只要拳頭大，

食物、女人都可以到手，

只要拳頭大，

其他人都要服從，

拳頭就是正義。

拳頭就是正義，人類互相殘殺，

放縱慾望，人類嚐到了苦果，

殺了別人，自己的親人也被殺害一類的，

父子相殘一類的，

冤冤相報，傷痛重複著、累積著。

人類害怕死亡，

害怕黑夜、閃電、月蝕，

人類活在恐懼之中。

「人類應該怎麼活？」

基於傷痛與恐懼，

有一個答案浮現了，

「人類應該聽神的話。」

於是有一個模糊的善的概念，

傳統價值是一個模糊的善。

參、傳統價值的特點。

從部落的巫師到君權神授，

傳統價值是「聽神的話」，

於是傳統價值有幾個特點：

一、傳統價值是服從。

人類應該服從神，

人民應該服從國王，

子女應該服從父母，

女人應該服從男人，

學生應該服從老師，

我們應該服從神、聖人、祖靈。

二、傳統價值反對質疑。

因為人類沒有找到善的理由，

傳統價值沒有理由，

　我的目標是：生命真的有意義

所以如果有學生問：

「為什麼我們應該聽聖人的話？」

老師沒有答案，答案是棍子。

三、傳統價值是保守。

傳統價值反對好奇心，

這是傳統價值的秘密，

傳統價值不會告訴你：

「傳統價值是基於恐懼與傷痛。」

他們只會說：

「這是基於老祖宗的智慧、經驗。」

或是什麼都不說，

反對新事物不需要任何理由。

四、傳統價值反對慾望。

弱肉強食、放縱慾望會帶來悲劇，

所以傳統價值反對慾望。

人有罪，人有原罪，

一直產生慾望的身體是罪惡的，

所以要用戒律來壓制這罪惡的身體。

五、傳統價值反對自私。

傳統價值鼓勵犧牲，

為了神犧牲，

為了國王而犧牲，

為了眾人而犧牲，

為了紳士精神而犧牲，

為了道德而犧牲，

利與義相衝突，

傳統價值是崇高而虛幻的價值。

肆、衝突。

傳統價值是過去的善，

從弱肉強食、放縱慾望中保護了人們。

但傳統價值也是邪惡的威權，

古老的教條形成枷鎖、巨牆，

囚禁著人們，

傳統價值壓迫著人們。

而因為傳統價值帶來了傷害，

所以被傷害的人們累積力量，

試著挑戰傳統價值，

於是出現了激烈的衝突。

一、君權神授。

忠誠是傳統價值，君權神授，

國王的正統性來自於上帝，

孔子也教導著忠誠，

佛教徒不生氣、不罵人，

不對國王生氣、不罵國王，

宗教教人像羔羊一樣順從。

而民主先烈喊著反抗與自由，

不要服從，要反抗，

民主是罵總統，

自由與忠誠曾經有很激烈的衝突。

二、聽父母的話。

孝順是傳統價值，在中華文化中，

孔子是所有老師的老師，

而孔子教導著孝順，

父母總是說：「我是為你好。」

然後控制、決定子女的人生，

甚至扼殺子女的人格，

天下無不是的父母，

就算父母真的是人渣，

在傳統價值之下，子女依然難以反抗，

傳統價值曾經逼許多人走上絕路。

為了突破這個枷鎖，

曾經發生了很激烈的衝突。

三、聽男人的話。

聽男人的話是傳統價值，

儒家教導著三從四德，

在家從父、出嫁從夫、夫死從子。

梵蒂岡中女性不能當神父，

佛教說女性的罪業較重、福報較少，

和梵蒂岡一樣，佛教男女不平等，

伊斯蘭教讓女性戴上了黑紗。

男女平等不是理所當然的，

男女平等的敵人是傳統價值。

四、奴隸。

犧牲奉獻是傳統價值，

人民應該為了國王犧牲、為了國家犧牲，只有國家、沒有個人、沒有人權。

國王高高在上，平民都應該犧牲，

傳統價值不是平等，

每個人都應該為了國王犧牲。

不只是制度，人民連靈魂都是國王的奴隸，為國王而死還覺得開心。

每個人都是國王、貴族、官員的奴隸，如果商人賺錢了，也會想買奴隸，也許買個黑人吧。

這就是傳統價值形成的風氣。

五、慾望。

去除慾望是傳統價值，

孔子說生命的意義是讀書然後報效國家，

佛陀和耶穌說生命的意義是回天堂，

除此之外的事都是沒有意義的，

慾望會污染人的靈魂，

你只能唱聖歌，你不可以唱搖滾樂，

讀經書會被讚美，看漫畫會被責罵，

你不可以打扮，你不可以有個人興趣，

重聖輕凡，職業是低俗次要的，修行是崇高的，如果有青少年想當搖滾樂手，他要用很大的力氣向父母抗爭。

六、保守。

保守是傳統價值，

傳統價值反對好奇心，當科學家說地球繞著太陽轉，教會生氣了，當人類要登陸月球，宗教害怕觸怒神。

宗教鼓勵背誦經典，如果你問：神會不會大便？天國的人談戀愛嗎？失戀會哭嗎？

傳統價值會對你的問題發怒，傳統價值不喜歡學生們發問，思考與教條曾經有激烈的衝突。

七、尊敬與畏懼。

尊敬神是傳統價值，

畏懼神也是傳統價值，

宗教在表達天堂的美好的同時，

也表達著地獄的恐怖，

寧可信其有，不可信其無，你不要膽大妄為，小心掉入地獄，道德來自於對地獄的恐懼。

天堂是美好的，而地球即將迎來世界末日，日常生活如泡沫般脆弱，只有天堂是永恆的，辭去工作，到聖山祈禱吧！

當有人夢想著找到好工作，和愛人相守一輩子，當有人不相信神，只想追求平凡時，宗教散播著恐懼，你應該感到恐懼，然後加入宗教。

而當有人要犧牲工作與家庭，他的家庭被迫陷入激烈的爭吵。

伍、普世價值。

因為傳統價值幫國王欺壓人民，幫男人控制女人，幫權貴畜養奴隸，傳統價值打壓科學與娛樂、思考與創作，所以被打壓的人們漸漸懷疑傳統價值，懷疑之後出現衝突，但衝突後人們有得到新價值嗎？「人類應該怎麼活？」這問題有答案了嗎？

人們喊出了新的價值，

因為傳統價值是忠誠、服從、犧牲、保守、教條，所以普世價值是自由、平等、人權、思考、質疑。

「人權」這個詞是為了對抗「犧牲」才被大喊，以前只有國家、沒有個人，每個人都該為了國家犧牲，為了阻止「犧牲」才有了「人權」。「自由」是為了對抗國王的壓迫，為了對抗「忠誠」才有了「自由」。「平等」是為了對抗「服從」，貴族、老師、男人教平民、學生、女人「服從是美德」。思考、好奇不是理所當然的，社會保守不喜歡新事物，「教條」與「質疑」是對立的，「聖人說」與「質疑」是對立的，為了對抗「傳統價值」所以人們喊出了「普世價值」。

人們喊出了普世價值，但普世價值的理由是什麼？

「為什麼忠誠是錯的？而自由是對的？」支持普世價值的人給出了奇怪的理由，

因為上帝支持自由，所以自由是對的。

自由「本來」就是對的，所有人都說是對的，所以是對的。

因為我沒有答案，我也不相信神的答案，人生沒有答案，所以每個人都可以發表（胡說）自己的看法，所以自由。

金恩博士說：「I have a dream.」，

平等與人權是沒有根據的夢想，

普世價值是一個主觀的看法，沒有根據，普世價值是一個謊言，沒有什麼是「本來」就是對的。

陸、筆者的答案。

生命的意義是人類歷史中最難的問題，

「人類應該怎麼活？」這問題一直沒有答案，人們只有價值、看法、夢想，而筆者找到答案了。

對照組不維護環境，實驗組維護環境，

這樣可以證明人類應該關心故鄉。

對照組讓志願者生活在空的房間，實驗組讓志願者生活在有娛樂、有電話的房間，這樣可以證明人的心會餓，人要思考、豐富心靈。

對照組的警報器會在水災來臨時說：「水災、水災、請趕快避難。」，實驗組的警報器只會說：「國王很偉大。」，這樣可以證明警報器應該屬於人民，忠誠錯了，監督才是對的。

「人類應該怎麼活？」筆者拿出證明了，

每個人都應該思考，每個人都應該關心故鄉。

柒、結語。

政治人物和學者們常常說：

「我們要改掉威權，

我們要走向進步的普世價值。」

真是奇怪，

思考與人權是普世的嗎？

為什麼以前人們不思考呢？

舊的觀念是什麼？

傳統價值是什麼？

傳統價值與普世價值起了怎樣的衝突？

美國常說：「願上帝保佑美國。」

美國常說：「捍衛普世價值。」

真是矛盾，

美國忘記了聖經和普世價值的衝突。

筆者證明了：「每個人都應該思考，

每個人都應該關心故鄉。」

「普世價值錯了，思考與人權是客觀的，

不是價值。」

這是筆者的發現，

全世界只有筆者堅定地挑戰了普世價值。

而在這篇文章，筆者說明了傳統價值，筆者也說明了普世價值是為了對抗傳統價值才出現的。

生命的意義與完整的答案

壹、前言。

「人類應該怎麼活？」

當筆者問 ChatGPT 生命有沒有意義？

ChatGPT 說有人認為有，有人認為沒有。

如果上維基百科找答案，維基百科有許多答案，那麼那個答案是真的？維基百科沒有說：「生命的意義這難題已經被解開了。」雖然維基百科不一定是對的，但學者們也沒有大聲地說生命的意義這難題已經被解開了。

筆者的故鄉是台灣，當選舉時，總統候選人喊著普世價值，台灣大學並沒有指正，台灣大學沒有說民主不是主觀的價值。

台灣有許多宗教，台灣人一邊拜著傳統價值，又一邊說民主價值很偉大，

耶穌、佛陀、孔子證明生命有意義了嗎？

民主、人權被證明了嗎？

老師們教著道德，老師們又說人生沒有標準答案，政治人物和學者們常說：「台灣人應該……」，他們是在唬爛、喊口號，還是這問題已經被解開了？

「人類應該怎麼活？」

這問題已經有答案了嗎？

一個完整的答案應該包含：

一、真的有答案了，和證明。

二、挑戰者。

三、和舊觀念的比較。

四、作者的思考歷程。

這只是基本功，但學者們只是胡說著：

「人類應該……」「台灣人應該……」，

所以在本篇文章，筆者將說明一個完整的答案應該包含：答案、理由、作者、過程、被解決的題目。

貳、真的和證明。

「人類應該怎麼活？」

這個問題有答案嗎？

學者們說：「人生沒有標準答案，

每個人都可以發表自己的看法。」

學者們在發表了各種答案後，

學者們說謊了，他們開始假裝自己有答案，老師喊著道德，老師教學生遵守道德，好像道德已經被證明了一樣。學者們喊著民主價值、普世價值，學者們說謊了，普世價值並不存在，主觀的價值沒有對與錯，沒有所有人都應該遵守的主觀價值，當美國總統喊著捍衛價值時，哈佛、史丹佛沒有開記者會糾正，哈佛、史丹佛並不清楚民主是主觀或客觀。

這是簡單的基本功，但學者們並沒有遵守，當說出一個答案，這個答案是真的或是看法？理由與證明方法呢？大聲喊著民主價值並不能證明什麼。

而在我的著作「為什麼你要聽我的話？從威權到自由到共好。」當中，

我準備了實驗組和對照組，當危急時，對照組的廣播器會大喊「危險、救命」，而實驗組的廣播器會大喊「國王好偉大」，筆者證

　我的目標是：生命真的有意義

明了廣播器應該屬於人民，筆者證明了民主，「普世價值錯了，民主是客觀的。」

　　人生有沒有答案？有沒有在未來永遠是對的事呢？人們說未來是未知，人們說人生沒有標準答案，在我的書「怎麼增加人類全體的財富？生命的意義與留給明天的財富」當中，我說明了：「明天是已知，生命有意義，只要人類還存活，人類就要維護環境、關心故鄉。」而學者們認為明天是未知，所以他們只能在未知中相信著「價值」，學者們胡說著「價值」，但一個完整的答案應該要具備「真的」、「證明方法」。

參、宣稱。

　　台灣的教育部長、文化部長常常說：

　　「台灣應該走向多元，台灣應該建立一個和諧、永續的社會。」

　　很多政治人物和學者說：

　　「台灣應該……」，

　　政治人物總是喜歡假裝自己對台灣的未來很有想法，文化部長必須讓自己看起來很有文化，但這些都不是完整的答案。

　　當文化部長炫耀著「台灣人應該怎麼活？」的答案，

　　當文化部長說：「台灣應該……」

　　他解開這個難題了嗎？

　　為什麼他沒有宣稱？

　　為什麼文化部長不是說：

　　「我解答了台灣人應該怎麼活這難題，

　　台灣應該……」？

如果這答案是文化部長自己想到的，

他應該宣稱他解開了這問題，

如果這答案不是文化部長想到的，

他應該說明出處，

他應該說明是誰挑戰了這個難題。

沒有出處、沒有宣稱的答案不是完整的答案，文化部忘記了台灣以前的茫然。

決長、我知道我解答了生命的意義這難題，我將我的答案寫成書出版，我將我的書用 email 寄給許多教授，在 2015 年 10 月，我花錢在報紙刊登了啟示，我宣稱：「我解答了生命的意義。」而我只有得到嘲笑，「有一個瘋子宣稱他解答了生命的意義」。這是一件基本的事，如果有答案了就應該宣稱有答案了，而我宣稱了，但學者們、教育部長、文化部長他們沒有宣稱。

肆、與舊觀念的比較。

台灣的教育部長常說：「台灣應該走向多元。」通識老師常常寫文章說：「學生應該思考。」而為什麼學生應該思考呢？通識老師說：「因為老師沒有人生的答案，所以學生應該思考。」但老師是笨蛋無法推論出學生應該思考，通識老師沒有好好說明「推導過程」，而除了「推導過程」之外，當老師拿出了「思考」這個答案時，題目是什麼？通識老師的文章挑戰了什麼題目？挑戰了什麼舊觀念？為什麼以前人們不思考？填鴨教育？是那些教育家支持填鴨教育？當通識老師喊著「自由」時，是誰反對著自由？沒文化的獨裁者反對自由？還是聖人歌頌的偉大君王反對自由？當通識老師喊著「男女平等」時，是誰反對男女平等？父權？誰是父權？父權是那個思想家？是那一本書？不敢罵孔子所以罵「父權」？當教育部長喊著「多元」時，是誰反對著多元？題目與答案是成對的，「思考、多元」背後的題目是什麼？如果沒有說明題目卻有答案，就不是完整的答案。

　　筆者挑戰了生命的意義，筆者發現人的心靈像「空白」，能思考、能創造，需要填入色彩，生命有意義，人應該思考、應該豐富心靈，生命的意義是「多元」。

　　筆者挑戰了生命的意義，筆者知道這是一個令人害怕的題目，人們害怕思考，害怕思考生命的意義，曾經有哲學家認真地挑戰這題目，但失敗、發瘋、自殺了，在筆者的書「我們應該成為怎樣的人？生命的意義與教育的目的」當中，筆者說明了：民主最大的敵人是什麼？民主最大的敵人就是「所有人都不思考、不反抗、不愛自己」，「生命沒意義，不要想太多，聽國王、聖人的話就好。」，筆者在拿出答案的同時，筆者說明了題目，筆者說明了人類害怕思考的那段過去，有成對的題目與答案才是完整的答案。

　　台灣的總統常說：「台灣應該走向多元。」但台灣的總統從來沒有說明「思考」與「聽聖人的話」的衝突，台灣的總統沒有說明歷史，沒有說明茫然的過去，台灣 NO.1，台灣「本來」就很偉大，台灣「本來」就應該走向多元。

伍、思考過程。

　　我的書「生命任意數」當中

　　有我的思考過程，

　　我在國一開始思考生命的意義，

　　那時候給自己一個狡辯的答案：

　　生命的意義就是尋找生命的意義。

後來我認為生命的意義是感動，

後來我認為是落實，

後來我認為是開創，

後來我認為是開創與安穩的調和，

後來我認為是百戰的磨練……

最後我發現了心的本質，

生命的意義是空白（多元），

這就是最後的答案了，

我那時就知道自己

已經找到最後的答案了，

心的創造力、雙手萬能，

不會有比萬能更好的答案了。

而書名是「生命任意數」，

就是「多元就只能是多元」。

生命的意義是聽神的話，

是犧牲奉獻，

是成聖成賢，

是功利賺錢，

是分數至上……

這些都是錯的，

答案是 1、2、3、4……

但 1、2、3、4……

都是錯的。

我的書中有過程不成熟的答案，

我的思路歷程，

一個完整的答案必須要包含

作者的思考過程。

當我聽到政治人物與學者說：

「台灣應該……」，

我很想知道他們從幾歲開始思考這問題，

有沒有過程不成熟的答案呢？

有沒有草稿跟花絮呢？

陸、結語。

「人類應該怎麼活？」

一個廣播器發出警告，

一個廣播器說「國王真偉大」，

筆者證明了民主是真的。

一個空的房間和一個有娛樂的房間，

可以證明人要豐富心靈，

對照組維護環境，

實驗組不維護環境，

可以證明人類應該關心故鄉，

筆者證明了「生命有意義」

「民主是真的」。

政治人物和學者們喊著「價值」，

寫著文章說：「台灣人應該……」，

這個「應該」是看法？還是真的？

證明方法呢？

這個「應該」是一個宣稱嗎？

這個「應該」挑戰了什麼舊觀念？

這個「應該」有草稿嗎？

一個完整的答案必須包含：

答案、真的與證明、挑戰者、

與舊觀念的比較、思考過程。

請學者們拿出完整的答案，

不要隨口說著「應該」。

生命的意義與筆者的目標

壹、前言。

人類有辦法飛上天空嗎？

如果你問 GhatGPT，

或是你問學校的任何一位老師，

他們會給你肯定的答案，然後

他們會告訴你萊特兄弟的故事。

人類有辦法登陸月球嗎？

如果你上維基百科，

或是你問學校的任何一位老師，

他們會給你肯定的答案，然後

你會聽到阿姆斯壯這個名字。

如果學生問：「生命有意義嗎？」

老師們不會堅定地回答：「有」，

老師們會擔心發問的學生是不是想自殺，

老師們會付出陪伴與勉勵，

老師們是無力的，

人類並沒有解答生命的意義。

決長、我曾經為「生命的意義」

這題目感到煎熬，

我的故鄉的台灣大學有學生

因為找不到生命的意義而自殺了。

現在，我已經證明生命有意義了，

我想告訴大家生命真的有意義，

但是台灣的總統、教育部長、
文化部長，他們阻擋著我，
本篇文章將說明：
「告訴大家生命真的有意義」
這個簡單的目標遇到了什麼阻擋。

本篇文章將說明：
一、決長的動機。
二、過去的矛盾。
三、決長的答案。
四、台灣的反應。

決長、我的目標是告訴大家：
「生命真的有意義。」
但台灣依然迴避著，
所以本篇文章要更尖銳地強調
「生命真的有意義。」

貳、決長的動機。

決長、我在國一的時候開始思考生命的意義，
不只是思考，而是煎熬，
生命沒意義嗎？
無論一個人怎麼努力，
達成多麼偉大的成就，
愛得多深，都只是夢幻泡影嗎？

那是冰冷而絕望的事，在絕望中，
我決定自己來找答案，
認真地讀書、認真地玩、
連混都認真地混，
但「自己找答案」
這想法只是一個詭辯，
生命依然沒有意義，
冰冷的絕望依然隱隱地令我煎熬，
決長我的目標是回答國中的我，
告訴國中的我：
「生命真的有意義。」

筆者曾經遇過這樣的事：
我深愛的人並不自愛，
那是一件傷心的事，
我想要告訴我深愛的人：
「生命有意義，
你應該要珍惜你自己。」
但這是一個謊言嗎？
我確定生命有意義了嗎？
「生命本來就有意義。」
「我覺得生命有意義。」，
「本來」和「我覺得」都是謊言，
決長我的目標是「生命真的有意義」。

我發現：當時的社會風氣不是熱情的，

人們的心是冰冷的，人們害怕著世界末日。支持民主的人大聲喊著：「覺醒、反抗。」有些支持民主的人將冰冷的心稱為「奴隸性」，社會是無聲的，人們心中已經放棄了，投票又如何，反正一樣爛，監督政府、關心社會又如何，歷史已經告訴我們，再怎麼偉大的王國也是走向滅亡，生命沒意義吧！再怎麼努力都是沒意義的吧！人們冰冷的心和筆者找不到生命的意義時的絕望感是相似的，支持民主的人重複地喊著：「覺醒、反抗。」，民主最大的敵人是：「所有人都不思考、不反抗、不愛自己。」，這是相同的題目，我想要告訴我深愛的人：「生命有意義，你應該珍惜你自己。」，民主是告訴人們：「生命有意義，你應該珍惜你自己，你應該關心故鄉（監督政府）。」，這也是我的目標，

決長我的目標是「生命真的有意義」。

參、過去的矛盾。

筆者的故鄉是台灣，台灣在中國的東南方，在二次世界大戰之後，蔣介石敗給了共產黨，蔣介石從中國帶了兩百萬人到台灣，在蔣介石的統治下，台灣人困惑自己是台灣人或中國人，讀著孔子的書，台灣人困惑自己是台灣人或中國人，可以不要讀孔子的書嗎？台灣的本土派夢想著新的價值，蔣介石實施威權統治，被迫害的人夢想著民主。

於是，本土派喊著：

「民主價值、台灣價值、普世價值。」

這是奇怪的事，本土派喊著台灣價值，但台灣應該還在找新的價值，台灣價值還沒有被找到。普世價值是奇怪的，人們找到一定是對的事了嗎？未知的未來，有人指出未來的方向了嗎？誰證明了普世價值？民主被證明了嗎？多數人決定和少數人決定，多數人依然走向茫然的未來。

學校的老師們也說著自我矛盾的話，

「善沒有標準答案，善與惡不是二元對立的。」真是奇怪，「善與惡不是二元對立」這句話是對的？是錯的？而老師們又教學生道德，善與惡又變得有標準答案了。

老師們說：「因為老師們沒有人生的答案，所以你應該思考。」真是奇怪，老師是笨蛋無法推導出學生應該思考。

思考一定是對的？

平庸、從眾一定是錯的？

老師說：「你應該愛自己、愛故鄉。」

但老師憑什麼逼別人愛國，

當有學生不願意學習、放縱慾望，

或是有學生將自己關在房間中，

或是有學生認為分數重要、愛不重要，

老師憑什麼改變別人的人生，

人類是無力的，老師們沒有辦法回答愛的理由，老師沒有找到一定是對的事，人類沒有找到未來的方向。

肆、筆者的答案。

決長、我的目標是「生命真的有意義」，

我認真地讀書、認真地玩、連混都認真地混，如果我燃燒一般地活著，也許我可以知道燃燒後是否留下了什麼。歡鬧後的寧靜，告別了一個階段的人生，我發現歡鬧後留下了感動，後來感動消失了，當感動消失後又留下了什麼？生命的意義真是可怕的題目，越是燃燒地活著，越覺得沒有留下什麼，寧靜越是可怕。

後來我發現了：「為什麼我在尋找著永恆？」，「生命的意義」這題目不應該是「天堂與永恆」，「生命的意義」是「人活著要做什麼？」，我發現人有心靈，像空白一樣，人能思考、創造，人的心靈會餓，人要為空白填入色彩。

　　我已經確定生命有意義了，人活著有一定要做的事，人的心靈會餓，人要思考、豐富心靈，為空白填入色彩，生命的意義是「多元」。

　　我的目標是告訴我愛的人：

　　「生命有意義，你應該珍惜你自己。」

　　但「人的心會餓、多元、為空白填入色彩」這個答案太抽象了，於是我寫了「心之共識」這本書，從「人的心會餓」變成「人會餓」，我要吃飯，你要吃飯，人無法拒絕吃飯，人類只有唯一的選擇，吃飯、珍惜地吃飯，人類活著有一定要做的事，生命的意義是「一起吃飯」。我回答了珍惜的理由，我回答了「為什麼我要管你？為什麼你也該管我？」，我說明了「人生有共同的答案」。

　　筆者已經解答了生命的意義，

　　飢餓是前進的理由，筆者找到了「人類未來該做的事」、「人類的方向」、「台灣的方向」、「確定的事」、「教育的目的」、「愛的理由」、「善的理由」。

伍、台灣的反應。

　　筆者的故鄉是台灣，為了對抗孔子，台灣尋找著台灣價值，但一直找不到，台灣的人民跟水牛有很深的感情，水牛辛苦工作、不怕吃苦，於是本土派說台灣價值是水牛精神，這是奇怪的事，對抗孔子的新答案是水牛，本土派矛盾地喊著水牛精神，又同時喊著「尋找台灣價值」，總統和教育部長喊著台灣價值，但又無法說明台灣價值是什麼。

　　而當我將我的書 email 給許多教授之後，

　　蔡英文總統突然喊著「幸福共好」、「台灣共好」，台灣價值是「多元、共好」。

共好是無名氏提出的（萬象當春是賴和），台灣價值是無名氏找到的，沒有理由，沒有尋找的過程，但本土派興高采烈地歡呼著，台灣有方向了，台灣要走向「多元」。

那生命有沒有意義呢？決長我的目標被蔡英文阻擋了。

當我努力告訴台灣人「生命的意義是多元」的時候，台北市議員苗博雅發起了一場公投，同性婚姻法的公投，苗博雅認為公投是對同性戀的支持，但這是奇怪的事，人權是用投票來決定的嗎？

跟苗博雅一起發起公投的幾位意見領袖中，有一個哲學老師。支持同性婚姻法的理由是什麼？同性婚姻法和「生命的意義」有關嗎？朱家安的「護家盟不萌」成為了當時挺同方的熱門書籍。

在「護家盟不萌」的開頭寫著，

朱家安不相信有人可以做到三件事：

一、找到生命的意義的最後答案。

二、證明那個答案。

三、逼朱家安吞下去。

朱家安說：「因為生命的意義不可能有答案，所以台灣應該走向多元。」

但生命沒有答案只會推導出台灣不一定要走向多元，「朱家安是笨蛋」無法推導出「台灣應該走向多元」。

朱家安剽竊了，朱家安沒有答案，朱家安認為不可能有答案，而他突然有「多元」這個答案。

決長我的目標是「生命有意義」，

但朱家安說生命沒意義，同性婚姻法沒有意義，沒有人可以逼別人吞下「同性婚姻法有意義」。

台灣突然喊著「多元」，

但生命依然沒有意義，

決長我的目標依然沒有實現。

陸、真的。

決長我的目標是：

「生命真的有意義，你應該珍惜你自己。」

也許老師們也害怕生命的意義這題目，

所以我縮小了我的目標，

從「生命真的有意義，你應該珍惜你自己」，改成「這是真的，
你應該珍惜你自己」。

對照組清醒玩賽車遊戲，

實驗組酒醉玩賽車遊戲，

這可以證明人應該清醒。

對照組不維護環境，

實驗組維護環境，

這可以證明人應該關心故鄉。

對照組的廣播器提出警告，

實驗組的廣播器說：「國王很偉大」，

這可以證明監督的重要，

這可以證明廣播器應該屬於人民，

我證明了民主。

對照組是沒有食物的房間，

實驗組是有食物的房間，

這可以證明人會餓。

對照組是空的房間，

實驗組是有娛樂、有手機的房間，

這可以證明人的心會餓，

人要思考、豐富心靈。

我把「生命的意義」這個詞丟掉，

我的新目標是：「這是真的，人活著有該做的事，人要思考、豐富心靈，關心故鄉。」這在一萬年後依然會是對的，而我已經提出證明了。

金恩博士說：「I have a dream.」

傳統價值、普世價值，

人們爭辯著價值。

台灣人應該愛台灣？

人可以自私嗎？

道德是價值、民主是價值。

多數決定、聽聖人的話，

誰能指出幸福的未來？

民主只是價值。

民主價值、台灣價值、普世價值，

人們一直這樣喊著，

而當我跟別人分享：

「普世價值錯了，

決長證明民主是客觀的」，

我只有聽到心碎的聲音。

柒、結語。

　　台灣的總統、教育部長把水牛精神丟掉了，現在他們說：「台灣應該走向多元。」但教育部長沒有說「生命真的有意義」。

　　台灣通過同性婚姻法了，

　　同性婚姻法是有意義的嗎？

　　同性婚姻法是對的嗎？

　　善沒有標準答案，

　　同性婚姻法不一定是對的，是嗎？

　　台灣喊著多元，

　　真的嗎？證明方法呢？誰證明了？

　　決長我的目標是「真的」，

　　為什麼教育部長喊著多元，

　　卻沒有證明方法？

　　台灣的總統把民主說成是價值，

　　台灣大學沒有出來糾正，

　　決長我的目標是「真的」，

　　請大聲說出來：

　　「普世價值錯了，

　　決長證明民主是真的」。

Preface

The author's hometown is Taiwan.

In the past, Taiwan believed in traditional values and Taiwan believed in the words of saints, but did the saints answer the meaning of life?

Some people say that life has meaning,

Some people say that life is meaningless, The saints have not proven.

The author has answered this most difficult question in human history. As long as an experimental group and a control group are prepared, it can prove that people have things they should do in life. Everyone should think and enrich their minds. The meaning of life is "diversity."

The author's goal is to tell everyone: life is really meaningful.

"Life is really meaningful, and the meaning of life is diversity ."

When the author shared this answer with Taiwanese people, Taiwan held a referendum on same-sex marriage laws. But is life meaningful? Taiwanese people still say paradoxically: There is no standard answer to goodness.

While Taiwanese are shouting for diversity, they also say that same-sex marriage laws are not necessarily correct.

The author said: Life "really" has meaning.

But Taiwan said: Same-sex marriage laws are not necessarily correct.

When the author shared the answer of "diversity" with Taiwan,

Taiwan's president went to many temples to kneel down to traditional values.

Taiwan's president shouted: "Taiwan's value is diversity."

Taiwan's President and Minister of Education's "diversity" is not a complete answer. Why is diversity right? Why are traditional values wrong? Method of proof, process of finding the answer, who found it? What about the claim that "people didn't have the answer before, but now I've found it." Has Taiwan found its direction?

Taiwan used to believe in traditional values;

Taiwan is now shouting about diversity,

But is Taiwan's diversity "real"?

Therefore, the content of this book includes these four topics:

"Same-Sex Marriage Laws and the Meaning of Life",

"The meaning of life and traditional values",

"The meaning of life and the complete answer",

"The meaning of life and the author's goal."

The author wants to tell everyone:

Life "really" has meaning.

Jue Chang

2024、06、21

Same-sex marriage laws and the meaning of life

Section 1 : Introduction.

The author's hometown is Taiwan, where same-sex marriage laws have been passed. In Asia, this is an incredible achievement. What's next then? Will Taiwan continue to hold pride parades? Absolutely, we will continue to cultivate culture and ideas.

"Humanity is debauched and fallen,

Now even same-sex marriage is allowed. Humanity has become even more debauched and fallen."

Some say so.

"The same-sex marriage law is a progress of human rights."

Some say so.

Who is right?

What's the reason?

Is there a standard answer to life?

This article will explain:

1. The reason for same-sex marriage laws.

2. Old concepts.

3. How to prove it?

4. The direction of the future.

There is no standard answer to life. Maybe the same-sex marriage law is progress? Maybe depravity? Yeah?

This article will explain: There is a standard answer to life, and the meaning of life is "diversity."

Section 2 : The reason for same-sex marriage laws.

Same-sex marriage laws were hard-won.

Many people took the courage to challenge old concepts.

That's why Taiwan has same-sex marriage laws.

Because same-sex marriage laws were hard-won, So, kids, we should support diversity.

Scholars teach the next generation this way.

What a strange thing!

Because those who support it work very hard,

So we should support same-sex marriage laws,

Then isn't it hard for the opposition?

"Because it is hard-won, everyone should support it." This is a completely illogical statement.

Taiwan's Ministry of Education shouted

"The value of diversity", But there is no right or wrong about values. Values are unfounded.

It's really strange,

Shout loudly about value,

But they didn't explain

reasons for same-sex marriage laws.

In this section, I will explain the reason for same-sex marriage laws.

What is the reason for same-sex marriage laws?

Is it "the value of diversity"?

No, same-sex marriage laws are not illusory values.

What is the reason for same-sex marriage laws?

The answer is very simple,

Because they just love each other,

They just simply want to be together,

So they hope to get married and get blessings from relatives and friends.

"Those who love each other can stay together."

That's the reason for same-sex marriage laws.

What is the reason for same-sex marriage laws? The answer is "love is the greatest".

If we delve deeper, the answer is: "they believe love is the greatest," and the reason is "they believe."

Section 3 : Old concepts.

"The same-sex marriage laws were hard-won ; many people took the courage to challenge old concepts."

So, what are the old concepts ?

Every December 25th,

Many people on earth celebrate Jesus' birthday, The Savior is born, born of a virgin. The Virgin Mary, who remained a virgin all her life, gave birth to Jesus.

Sex is bad,

Jesus was not born after his parents had sex.

There is the story of Adam and Eve in Genesis, Humans were kicked out of the Garden of Eden because they ate the forbidden fruit. In the book of Revelation, there is a great adulteress who brings disasters.

The meaning of life is to listen to God's words. The Bible teaches people to keep chastity, and lust is a sin that offends God.

Buddha said the meaning of life is to return to Buddha's Blessed Paradise.

Emotions, desires, enjoyment, beautiful women, food, and music are all dust that clouds the soul. People should purify their eyes, ears, noses, tongues, bodies, and minds. Contemplating the True Nature of the Mind.

Buddhism also teaches people to keep chastity;

Fornication is a sin against the commandments. If you commit fornication,

Will fall into hell, and the soul will suffer eternal pain.

Confucius said: A king should behave like a king, ministers should behave like ministers, a father should behave like a father, and children should behave like children.

The meaning of life is loyalty, we must listen to the words of the king and parents, and then contribute to the country,

Women should be loyal to men, obeying their fathers at home, their husbands when they get married, and their sons after their husbands die.

Confucius said: We must be gentlemen, not beasts.

"Ritual" is the foundation of a nation. Based on "ritual," people should observe chastity. The nation will erect monuments to commemorate women who remain chaste and do not remarry for life. If "ritual" is lost, the nation will perish in promiscuity and corruption.

In the old concept,

When teenagers say they want to be professional e-sports players when they grow up, parents with Confucian ideas will object.

Because playing is something that does not contribute to the country.

When teenagers say they want to be rock musicians when they grow up, their Buddhist-minded parents will object.

Because rock music can blind the soul.

When a nun wishes to wear beautiful clothes, the priest will oppose it because beautiful clothing is a temptation from Satan.

Personal interests, play, music, and clothes were all suppressed;

What about free love?

Religion does not encourage teenagers to engage in romantic relationships.

Maybe young people don't consider dating to be a significant issue, but parents are very worried. They are not worried about sexually transmitted diseases or pregnancy, but worried that if the soul is sinned, the soul will be punished forever.

They are also worried about the end of the world and the final judgment.

Many people misunderstand and believe that religion opposes same-sex marriage. However, even when it comes to heterosexual teenagers dating, religion expresses concerns.

Is it right for love to bring people together?

No, people should restrain their desires. Lust and corruption will destroy mankind.

Section 4 : Doubt and resistance.

The meaning of life is to return to heaven. When teenagers engage in romantic relationships and fall in love, whether with the opposite sex or the same sex, parents become worried. And if there are teenagers who fall in love with the same sex, they may be forced to undergo treatment and correction.

Love should be together, right?

When someone falls in love with someone of the same sex,

They were confused, The love in their hearts conflicts with the morality in their minds. Should they obey morality and be good children loved by their parents and Jesus, or should they obey the love in their hearts?

They blame themselves, feel conflicted, helpless, guilty, and hope to be understood.

They experienced a long silent time,

hiding, Can't be in the sun. They doubt themselves, they feel guilty, and they cannot voice their opinions.

When they accumulate strength and voice their opinions, They said the same word as the democratic martyrs:

"Freedom"

The democratic martyrs fought for freedom from the king,

 我的目標是：生命真的有意義

And they followed the answer of the democratic martyrs :

We are free, and it is our freedom to be with the people we love. Please refrain from interfering with our freedom.

"Good and evil are not binary opposites."

There is no standard answer to good and evil, and there is no standard answer to life. Please don't impose morality on us.

Based on "freedom" and "the freedom of lovers to be together", some places have passed same-sex marriage laws.

Section 5 : The shortcomings of freedom.

Based on freedom, lovers have the freedom to marry,

But are same-sex marriage laws ethical?

Don't know, they just want to be together,

They were not challenging Jesus.

Do same-sex marriage laws represent decadence?

Do same-sex marriage laws represent progress?

Don't know,

There are no standard answers to life.

Should we teach the next generation traditional values?

Should we teach the next generation the value of diversity?

Don't know,

Value is subjective and unfounded;

The future is unknown,

Teachers aren't sure what's good for the next generation;

No one has found something that is definitely right,

No one has found something that will be right in the future.

Do humans know what kind of future humans should move towards?

No, religion says the meaning of life is to return to heaven.

And philosophers say there is no standard answer to the meaning of life.

The Pride Parade is a slogan-chanting event.

What are the old concepts?

Why are old concepts wrong?

Why do same-sex marriage laws represent progress?

They didn't answer the questions,

They just chant slogans.

Section 6 : The author's answer.

The meaning of life is the most difficult question in human history. The future is unknown and no one can point out the direction of the future.

The author answered this question and prepared experimental methods:

As long as we prepare an experimental group that maintains the environment and a control group that does not maintain the environment, it can be proved that humans must maintain the environment. This is something humans must continue to do.

As long as the water and electricity are cut off, It can be proved that people must care about their hometown, this is something that humans must continue to do.

As long as the experimental group and the control group are prepared, the farmers and shops in the control group work normally, and the farmers and shops in the experimental group go on strike, it can be proved that people must cooperate and people must cooperate to eat together.

As long as we prepare an empty room and a room with entertainment and mobile phones, it can prove that people have emotional needs. Human beings must think and enrich their minds. Human beings need love and laughter.

Just prepare the food you like and a hundred volunteers, and observe whether all volunteers like the food. This can prove that people have similarities and differences, and this is also a similarity. Everyone must think about it. Everyone must recognize their own differences.

These are things that humans must continue to do, are the direction of the future, and are the answers to the meaning of life.

The author challenged Jesus, Buddha, and Confucius,

Confucius said that the meaning of life is loyalty, and women must be loyal to men. Confucius was wrong, loyalty was wrong, thinking is right.

The Bible says that the meaning of life is to remain chaste and return to the Garden of Eden. The Bible is wrong, the earth is humanity's only home.

The Buddha said that emotions and desires are dust that cloud the mind.

Buddha was wrong, human beings need love and laughter.

The meaning of life is diversity,

Think, fill in love and laughter, enrich the mind, increase the perspective of appreciating beauty.

This is what humans must continue to do, and this is the direction of
the future.

Section 7 : The direction of Taiwan.

Taiwan once held a referendum on same-sex marriage laws, and
they shouted "diversity." They said: good and evil are not binary
opposites. There is no standard answer to life, so we must be diverse.

It's really a contradiction. There is no standard answer to good and
evil, so you can vote for it or you can vote against it. There is no standard
answer to good and evil. Maybe we should pass same-sex marriage laws.
Maybe we should oppose same-sex marriage laws to protect teenagers.
"There is no standard answer to good and evil." This cannot deduce the
direction of Taiwan.

And when the author said: "I have solved the meaning of life, the
meaning of life is diversity."

Taiwan laughed at the author, "It's ridiculous, there is no answer to
the meaning of life." Then they said that Taiwan has a direction, and
Taiwan's future must be diversity.

They didn't challenge Jesus, they didn't answer the question of the
future,

Taiwan's direction does not fall from the sky. The author proves that
Taiwan should move towards diversity.

 我的目標是：生命真的有意義

Section 8 : Conclusion.

Taiwan has passed same-sex marriage laws.

The next step is education.

Same-sex marriage laws are a breakthrough and progress.

So what are the old beliefs?

Why are old ideas wrong?

What is the reason for diversity? how to prove?

Why doesn't diversity represent depravity?

Why does diversity represent progress?

Please say it out loud!

The future has a direction,

Jue Chang answers the meaning of life,

The meaning of life is "diversity".

The Meaning of Life and Traditional Values

Section 1 : Introduction.

The author's hometown is Taiwan.

Taiwan used to be authoritarian;

Taiwan is now moving towards democracy,

Academics and politicians shouted:

"We should get rid of authoritarianism,

We should move towards progressive universal values".

It's really strange,

Are universal values universal?

There are many religions in Taiwan. When elections are held,

The president will visit every temple,

The saints from thousands of years ago were so great,

The wisdom of our ancestors is so great,

The president knelt down,

It's really strange,

The wisdom of thousands of years ago is so great,

And we should move towards progressive universal values.

This is a contradiction.

This article will explain:

1. Traditional values.

2. Conflict of values.

3. Universal value.

 我的目標是：生命真的有意義

4. The author's answer.

"How should humans live?

What kind of future should we move towards? "

Is there an answer to this question?

What were the old answers?

What are the new ideas?

What's the conflict?

This article will explain traditional values.

This article will illustrate the conflict.

Section 2 : Traditional values.

"How should humans live?"

This is not a question that one is born knowing.

Well, there's no need to think too much.

The answer is "Be the strong one, the strong one can eat the weak one."

As long as your fist is big,

Food and women are available,

As long as your fist is big,

Everyone else must obey,

The fist is justice.

Fist is justice, humans kill each other.

Indulging desires, human beings taste the bitter consequences.

If you kill others, your own relatives may also be killed.

Or something like father and son killing each other,

Injury for injury, and pain is repeated and accumulated.

Humans are afraid of death,

Afraid of night, lightning, lunar eclipse,

Humanity lives in fear.

"How should humans live?"

Based on pain and fear,

An answer emerged,

"Humans should listen to God."

So there is a vague concept of goodness,

Traditional values are a vague good.

Section 3 : Characteristics of traditional values.

From tribal wizards to divine right of kings,

The traditional values are "listen to the word of God",

Therefore, traditional values have several characteristics:

1. Traditional values are obedience.

Humans should obey God,

People should obey their king,

Children should obey their parents,

Women should obey men,

Students should obey their teachers,

We should obey gods, saints, and ancestral spirits.

2. Traditional values are against questioning.

Because humans have not found a reason to be good,

There is no reason for traditional values;

So if a student asks:

"Why should we listen to the saints?"

The teacher has no answer, the answer is a stick.

3. Traditional values are conservative.

Traditional values are against curiosity,

This is the secret of traditional values,

Traditional values don't tell you:

"Traditional values are based on fear and pain."

They will only say:

"This is based on the wisdom and experience of our ancestors."

Or say nothing,

They don't need any reason to be against something new.

4. Traditional values are against desire.

The strong eating the weak and indulging in desires will bring tragedy.

So traditional values are against desire.

Humanity is guilty, humanity has original sin,

A body that constantly produces desires is sinful;

Therefore, this sinful body should be suppressed by commandments.

5. Traditional values are against selfishness.

Traditional values encourage sacrifice;

Sacrifice for God,

Sacrifice for the king,

Sacrifice for the group,

Sacrifice for the gentlemanly spirit,

Sacrifice for morality,

Profit and justice conflict,

Traditional values are lofty and illusory values.

Section 4 : Conflict.

Traditional values are the goodness of the past;

Protected people from "the strong eating the weak and indulging desires".

But traditional values are also evil authoritarians;

Ancient dogmas form shackles and great walls,

Imprisoning people,

Traditional values oppress people.

And because traditional values have caused harm,

So people who have been hurt accumulate strength,

Try to challenge traditional values,

Fierce conflicts ensued.

1. The divine right of kings.

Loyalty is a traditional value,

Divine right of kings,

The king's legitimacy comes from God,

Confucius also taught loyalty,

Buddhists do not get angry or curse;

Don't be angry with the king, don't curse the king,

Religion teaches people to be obedient like lambs.

And the democratic martyrs shouted for resistance and freedom,

Resist, don't obey,

Democracy means criticizing the president;

There was a fierce conflict between freedom and loyalty.

2. Listen to your parents.

Listening to parents is a traditional value. In Chinese culture,

Confucius is the teacher of all teachers,

Confucius taught to listen to your parents,

Parents always say:

"I'm doing this for your own good."

Then control and decide the lives of their children,

Even kill the personality of the children.

There are no bad parents in the world,

Even if your parents are really scum,

Under traditional values, it is still difficult for children to resist,

Traditional values once drove many people to a dead end.

In order to break through this shackles,

There were fierce conflicts.

3. Listen to men.

Listening to men is a traditional value,

Confucius taught women to listen to men,

At home, a woman obeys her father. After she gets married, she obeys her husband. After her husband dies, a woman obeys her son.

Women cannot be priests in the Vatican;

Buddhism says that women have heavier sins and less blessings.

Like the Vatican, there is no equality between men and women in Buddhism;

Islam makes women wear black veils.

Equality between men and women is not a matter of course;

The enemy of gender equality is traditional values.

4. Slaves.

Sacrifice and dedication are traditional values,

People should sacrifice for the king and the country. There is only the country, no individuals, and no human rights.

Traditional values are not equality;

Everyone should die for the king.

Not only the political system, but also the souls of the people are the slaves of the king, and they feel happy even if they die for the king.

Everyone is a slave to the king, nobles, and officials. If a businessman makes money, he will also want to buy a slave, maybe a black man.

This is the atmosphere created by traditional values.

5. Desire.

Eliminating desires is a traditional value;

Confucius said that the meaning of life is to study and then serve the country.

Buddha and Jesus said that the meaning of life is to return to heaven,

Everything else is meaningless,

Desire pollutes the human soul,

You can only sing hymns, you can't sing rock music,

If you read the Bible you will be praised, if you read comics you will be scolded.

You can't dress up, you can't have personal interests,

Emphasis on the holy and despise the ordinary,

Occupation is vulgar and secondary, while spiritual practice is noble. If a teenager wants to be a rock musician, he will have to fight hard against his parents.

6. Conservative.

Conservatism is a traditional value,

Traditional values oppose curiosity. When scientists say that the earth revolves around the sun, the church gets angry. When humans want to land on the moon, religions are afraid of offending God. Religion encourages memorizing scriptures. If you ask: Does God poop? Do people in heaven fall in love? Will people in heaven cry when they are heartbroken?

Traditional values will get angry at your questions. Traditional values don't like students asking questions. There has been intense conflicts between thinking and dogma.

7. Respect and fear.

Respecting God is a traditional value;

Fear of God is also a traditional value;

While religion expresses the beauty of heaven,

It also expresses the horror of hell,

It is better to believe that something exists than to believe that something does not exist. Don't be daring and be careful about falling into hell. Morality comes from the fear of hell.

Heaven is beautiful, but the earth is about to usher in the end of the world. Daily life is as fragile as a bubble. Only heaven is eternal. Quit your job and go to the Holy Mountain to pray!

When someone dreams of finding a good job and spending a lifetime with his lover, when someone does not believe in God and just wants to pursue the ordinary, religion spreads fear. You should feel fear and then join the religion. And when someone wants to sacrifice work and family, his family is forced into a fierce quarrel.

Section 5 : Universal value.

Because traditional values help kings oppress the people, help men control women, and help the powerful raise slaves, traditional values suppress science and entertainment, thinking and creation, so the suppressed people gradually doubt traditional values, and conflicts arise after doubts. But do people have new values after conflict? "How should humans live?" Is there an answer to this question?

People shouted new values,

Because traditional values are loyalty, obedience, sacrifice, conservatism, and dogma,

 我的目標是：生命真的有意義

So universal values are freedom, equality, human rights, thinking, and questioning.

The word "human rights" was shouted to counter "sacrifice". In the past, there was only the country and no individual. Everyone should sacrifice for the country.

In order to prevent "sacrifice", "human rights" were created.

"Freedom" is to fight against the oppression of the king,

To fight against "loyalty" comes "freedom".

"Equality" is to combat "obedience". Nobles, teachers, and men teach civilians, students, and women that "obedience is a virtue."

Thinking and curiosity are not taken for granted;

Society is conservative and doesn't like new things;

"Dogma" and "questioning" are opposites.

"Saint said" is the opposite of "questioning". In order to fight against "traditional values", people shout "universal values".

People shout out universal values,

But what is the rationale for universal values? "Why is loyalty wrong? Why freedom is right?" People who support universal values give strange reasons,

Because God supports freedom, freedom is right.

Freedom is "originally" right. Everyone says it is right, so it is right.

Because I don't have the answer, and I don't believe in God's answer. There is no answer in life, so everyone can express and talk nonsense about their own opinions, so they are free.

Dr. King said: "I have a dream."

Equality and human rights are baseless dreams;

Universal value is a subjective view with no basis. Universal value is a lie. Nothing is "originally" right.

Section 6 : The author's answer.

The meaning of life is the most difficult question in human history,

"How should humans live?" This question has never been answered. People only have values, opinions, and dreams, and the author has found the answer.

The control group did not maintain the environment;

The experimental group maintains the environment,

This proves that humans should care about their hometown.

The control group asked a volunteer to live in an empty room.

The experimental group asked a volunteer to live in a room with entertainment and a mobile phone.

This can prove that people's hearts will be hungry, and people need to think and enrich their minds.

The broadcaster in the control group would say: "Flood, flood, please evacuate quickly." When the flood came, the broadcaster in the experimental group would only say: "The king is great." This can prove that the broadcaster should belong to the people, and loyalty is wrong , supervision is right.

"How should humans live?" The author provided proof,

Everyone should think and enrich their minds, and everyone should care about their hometown.

Section 7 : Conclusion.

Politicians and academics often say:

"We should get rid of authoritarianism,

We should move towards progressive universal values. "

It's really strange,

Are thinking and human rights universal?

Why were people afraid to think before?

What are the old ideas?

What are traditional values?

How did traditional values conflict with universal values?

The United States often says, "May God bless America."

The United States often says: "Defend universal values."

It's really a contradiction,

America has forgotten the conflict between the Bible and universal values.

The author proves: "Everyone should think,

Everyone should care about their hometown. "

"Universal values are wrong, thinking and human rights are objective.

Not value. "

This is what I found,

I am the only person in the world who has firmly challenged universal values.

In this article, the author explains traditional values, and the author also explains that universal values emerged to counter traditional values.

The Meaning of Life and the Complete Answer

Section 1 : Introduction.

"How should humans live?"

When the author asked ChatGPT, does life have meaning?

ChatGPT said that some people think there is, and some think there is not.

If you go to Wikipedia to find the answer, and Wikipedia has many answers, which answer is true? Wikipedia doesn't say :

"The difficult question of the meaning of life has been solved." Although Wikipedia is not necessarily right, scholars are not saying loudly that the difficult question of the meaning of life has been solved.

The author's hometown is Taiwan.

During the elections, the presidential candidates were all shouting out universal values. National Taiwan University did not correct it. They did not say that democracy is not a subjective value.

There are many religions in Taiwan;

Taiwanese people worship traditional values;

At the same time, Taiwanese people said that the value of democracy is great,

Did Jesus, Buddha, and Confucius prove that life has meaning?

Have democracy and human rights been proven?

Teachers teach morality, and teachers also say that there is no standard answer to life.

Politicians and scholars often say: "Taiwanese people should..." Are they bluffing and shouting slogans, or has this question been solved?

"How should humans live?"

Has this question been proven?

A complete answer should contain:

1. Reality and proof.

2. Challenger.

3. The comparison with old concepts.

4. The author's thinking process.

It's a simple thing, but scholars are just talking nonsense:

"Humans should..." "Taiwanese people should..."

So in this article, the author will explain that a complete answer should include: answer, reason, author, process, and challenged question.

Section 2 : Reality and proof.

"How should humans live?"

Is there an answer to this question?

Scholars say: "There is no standard answer to life.

Everyone can express their opinion. "

After scholars published various answers,

Scholars lied, they started pretending they had the answers, teachers shouted morals, teachers taught students to abide by morals as if morals had been proven.

Scholars shouted about democratic values and universal values. Scholars lied. Universal values do not exist. There is no right or wrong in subjective values. There are no subjective values that everyone should abide by. When the President of the United States shouted to defend values, Harvard and Stanford did not hold a press conference to correct the situation. Harvard and Stanford do not know whether democracy is subjective or objective.

It's a simple thing, but scholars don't follow it, when telling an answer, is the answer true or is it an opinion? What are the reasons and methods of proof? Shouting democratic values doesn't prove anything.

And in my book "Why do you have to listen to me? From authority to freedom to go to prosper together."

I prepared an experimental group and a control group,

When there is an emergency, the broadcaster in the control group will shout "Danger, help!"

The experimental group's broadcaster will shout "The King is so great." The author proves that the broadcasters should belong to the people, and the author proves democracy, "universal values are wrong, and democracy is objective."

Does life have an answer? Is there anything that will always be right in the future? People say that the future is unknown, and people say that there is no standard answer to life.

In my book " How to increase the wealth of all human beings? The meaning of life and the wealth left to tomorrow. " ,

I explained: "Tomorrow is known, and life has meaning. As long as humans still survive, humans must protect the environment and care about their hometown."

Scholars consider tomorrow to be unknown, So they can only

believe in "value" in the unknown. Scholars talk nonsense about "value", but a complete answer should have "reality" and "proof method".

Section 3 : Claim.

Taiwan's Minister of Education and Minister of Culture often say:

"Taiwan should move toward diversity, and Taiwan should build a harmonious and sustainable society."

Many politicians and scholars said:

"Taiwan should...", Politicians always like to pretend that they have great ideas about Taiwan's future, and the culture minister must make herself look cultured, but these are not complete answers.

When the Minister of Culture showed off the answer to "How should Taiwanese live?"

When the Minister of Culture said: "Taiwan should..."

Has she solved the question ?

Why didn't she claim it?

Why didn't the Minister of Culture say:

"I have solved the difficult question of how Taiwanese people should live.

Taiwan should ..."?

If this answer comes from the Minister of Culture herself,

She should claim that she has solved the question ,

If the answer is not from the Minister of Culture,

She should explain the source,

She should explain who challenged the question.

An answer without a source or claim is not a complete answer. The Minister of Culture has forgotten Taiwan's confused era.

Jue Chang, I know that I have solved the difficult question of the meaning of life. I wrote my answer into a book and published it. I sent my book to many professors by email. In October 2015,

I paid to publish the revelation in the newspaper,

I claim: I have answered the meaning of life.

And all I got was ridicule, "There is a madman who claims to have solved the meaning of life."

This is a basic thing. If you have the answer, you should claim that you have the answer. And I have claimed it, but the scholars, the Minister of Education, and the Minister of Culture have not claimed it.

Section 4 : Comparison with old concepts.

Taiwan's Minister of Education often says: "Taiwan should move towards diversity." General education teachers often write articles saying: "Students should think." And why should students think? General education teachers say: "Because teachers don't have the answers to life, students should think."

But the fact that teachers are idiots does not explain why students should think.

The general education teachers did not explain the "derivation process" well. In addition to the "derivation process", when the teachers came up with the answer of "thinking", what was the question? What topics do the general education teachers' articles challenge?

What old ideas are challenged?

Why didn't people think before?

Memorization-based education?

Which educators support memorization-based education?

When general education teachers shout "freedom", who is against freedom? Is it the illiterate dictator against freedom? Or are the great kings sung by saints opposed to freedom?

When general education teachers shout "equality between men and women", who is against equality between men and women?

Male-dominated thinking? Who supports Male-dominated thinking? Which thinkers are they? Which books are they? Is Confucius one of them?

When the Minister of Education shouts "diversity", who is against diversity? The questions and answers are paired. What is the question behind "Thinking, Diversity"? If there is no description of the question but there is an answer, it is not a complete answer.

The author challenged the meaning of life. The author found that the human mind is like a "blank". It can think and create and needs to be filled with color. Life is meaningful. People should think and enrich their minds. The meaning of life is "diversity".

The author challenges the meaning of life. I know this is a scary topic.

People are afraid to think,

People are afraid to think about the meaning of life;

There were philosophers who seriously challenged this topic, but failed, went crazy, and committed suicide.

In the author's book " What Kind of People Should We Be? The Meaning of Life and the Purpose of Education," the author explains:

What is the greatest enemy of democracy? The greatest enemy of democracy is "Everyone doesn't think, doesn't resist, not loving themselves." "Life is meaningless, don't think too much, just listen to the king and the saint."

While the author came up with the answer, the author explained the question,

The author explains the past that humans are afraid to think.

A complete answer consists of a paired question and answer.

Taiwan's president often says: "Taiwan should move toward diversity." However, Taiwan's president has never explained the conflict between "thinking" and "listening to the words of the saints."

Taiwan's president did not explain history;

There is no explanation of the confused past, Taiwan No.1, Taiwan is "originally" great, and Taiwan "originally" should move toward diversity.

Section 5 : Thinking process.

In my book "The Arbitrary Number In Life",

There is my thought process,

I started thinking about the meaning of life when I was in the first grade of junior high school.

At that time, I gave myself an evasive answer: The meaning of life is to find the meaning of life.

Later I thought that the meaning of life was heartwarming,

Later I thought it was implementation,

Later I thought it was to create,

Later I thought it was the harmony of creation and stability,

Later I thought it was my trained self……

Finally I discovered the nature of the heart,

The meaning of life is blank (diversity),

This is the final answer,

I know that I've found the final answer,

The creativity of the heart, the versatility of the hands, there can be no better answer than versatility.

The title of the book is "The Arbitrary Number In Life",

That is, "diversity can only be diversity."

The meaning of life is to listen to God's words,

It is sacrifice and dedication,

It is to become a sage and become a virtuous person ,

It's all about money ,

It's all about scores...

These are all wrong,

The answer is 1, 2, 3, 4……

But 1, 2, 3, 4... are all wrong.

My book contains answers that are half-baked in the thought process,

My thought process,

A complete answer must include

The author's thought process.

When I hear politicians and academics say:

"Taiwan should...",

I wonder at what age they started thinking about this?

Are there any immature answers?

Are there any drafts or behind-the-scenes details?

Section 6 : Conclusion.

"How should humans live?"

A broadcaster sounded a warning,

A broadcaster said, "The King is great,"

The author proves that democracy is real.

An empty room and a room with entertainment,

It can prove that people should enrich their minds.

The control group maintains the environment,

The experimental group does not maintain the environment;

It can prove that human beings should care about their hometown,

The author proves that "life has meaning"

"Democracy is real."

Politicians and academics shout about "value";

They wrote articles saying: "Taiwanese people should...",

Is this "should" an opinion? Or is it true?

What's the proof method?

Is this "should" a claim?

What old ideas does this "should" challenge?

Is there a draft for this "should"?

A complete answer must contain:

Answer, Reality and proof, Challenger,

Comparison with old ideas, Thought process.

Scholars, please provide complete answers,

Don't say "should" casually.

The Meaning of Life and the Author's Goal.

Section 1 : Introduction.

Is it possible for humans to fly into the sky?

If you ask GhatGPT,

Or you ask any teacher in school,

They will give you a definite answer and then

They will tell you the story of the Wright brothers.

Is there a way for humans to land on the moon?

If you go to Wikipedia,

Or you ask any teacher in school,

They will give you a definite answer and then

You'll hear the name Armstrong.

If a student asks: "Is life meaningful?"

Teachers will not answer firmly: "Yes",

Teachers will worry about whether the student who asked the question wants to commit suicide. Teachers will provide companionship and encouragement, Teachers are helpless; Humanity has not solved the meaning of life.

Jue Chang, I have experienced anguish over the question of "the meaning of life."

In my hometown,

Some students at National Taiwan University committed suicide because they could not find the meaning of life.

　我的目標是：生命真的有意義

Now, I have proven that life has meaning,

I want to tell everyone that life is really meaningful,

However, Taiwan's President, Minister of Education, Minister of Culture, they are blocking me,

This article will explain:

"Tell everyone that life is really meaningful"

What stands in the way of this simple goal.

This article will explain:

1. The author's motivation.

2. Contradictions in the past.

3. The author's answer.

4. Taiwan's reaction.

Jue Chang, my goal is to tell everyone:

"Life really has meaning."

But Taiwan still avoids it,

Therefore, this article will emphasize more pointedly

"Life really has meaning."

Section 2 : The author's motivation.

Jue Chang, I started thinking about the meaning of life when I was in the first grade of junior high school.

Not just thinking, but suffering,

Is life meaningless?

No matter how hard a person tries,

What a great achievement,

No matter how deep you love, are love, hard work and achievements just illusory dreams?

It was a cold and desperate thing. In despair,

I decided to find the answer myself,

I studied hard, played hard,

I even took idling time seriously.

But "find the answer myself"

This idea is just a sophistry,

Life is still meaningless,

The cold despair still tortures me,

Jue Chang, my goal is to answer my 12-year-old self, to tell my past self: "life is really meaningful".

The author once encountered such a thing:

The person I love deeply does not love herself,

That's a sad thing,

I want to tell the person I love deeply:

"Life has meaning,

You should cherish yourself. "

But is this a lie?

Am I sure life has meaning?

"Life is originally meaningful."

"I think life is meaningful.",

"Originally" and "I think" are both lies. Jue Chang, my goal is

　我的目標是：生命真的有意義

"life is really meaningful".

I found: the social atmosphere at that time was not enthusiastic;

People's hearts are cold, and people are afraid of the end of the world.

People who support democracy shout loudly: "Awaken and resist." Some people who support democracy call the cold hearts "servility."

Society is silent, people have given up in their hearts, So what about voting, it's just as bad anyway, so what about supervising the government and caring about society, history has told us that no matter how great a kingdom is, it will perish, and life is meaningless! No matter how hard you try, it's meaningless!

People's cold hearts are similar to the author's sense of despair when I can't find the meaning of life.

People who support democracy repeatedly shout: "Awaken and resist."

The biggest enemy of democracy is: "Everyone doesn't think, doesn't resist, not loving themselves."

This is the same topic. I want to tell the people I love deeply: "Life is meaningful, you should cherish yourself." Democracy is to tell people: "Life is meaningful, you should cherish yourself, and you should care about your hometown (Supervise the government)", this is also my goal,

Jue Chang, my goal is

"life is really meaningful".

Section 3 : Contradictions in the past.

The author's hometown is Taiwan, which is located to the southeast of China. After World War II, Chiang Kai-shek was defeated by the Communists. Chiang Kai-shek brought two million people from China to Taiwan. Under Chiang Kai-shek's rule, Taiwanese people were confused whether they were Taiwanese or Chinese. Reading Confucius's books, Taiwanese people are confused whether they are Taiwanese or Chinese. Is it possible not to read Confucius's books? The localists in Taiwan dream of new values. Chiang Kai-shek implemented authoritarian rule, and the persecuted people dreamed of democracy.

So the localists were shouting, "Democratic values, Taiwan's values, Universal values."

This is a strange thing. The localists are shouting about Taiwan's value, but Taiwan should still be looking for new value. Taiwan's value has not been found yet.

Universal values are strange. Have people found something that is definitely right? In the unknown future, has anyone pointed out the direction for the future? Who proves universal value? Has democracy been proven?

Is the majority decision always right?

The majority is still heading towards an uncertain future.

The teachers at the school also said self-contradictory words,

"There is no standard answer to good. Good and evil are not binary opposites." It's really strange. Is this sentence "Good and evil are not binary opposites" correct? Is it wrong? And teachers teach students morality, Suddenly there are standard answers to good and evil.

Teachers say, "Because teachers don't have the answers to life, you should think."

It's really strange,

"Teachers are stupid" cannot deduce that students should think.

Thinking must be right?

Is mediocrity and conformity necessarily wrong?

The teacher said: "You should love yourself and your hometown."

But why do teachers force others to be patriotic? When there are students who are unwilling to study and indulge their desires,

Or some students lock themselves in their rooms,

Or some students think that grades are important and love is not.

Or some students think that money is important and love is not.

Why can a teacher change other people's lives?

Human beings are helpless. Teachers cannot answer the reasons for love.

The teachers didn't find something that was definitely right;

Human beings have not found the direction for the future.

Section 4 : The author's answer.

Jue Chang, my goal is

"life is really meaningful".

I studied hard, played hard,

I even took idling time seriously.

If I live like burning, maybe I can know whether there is anything left after burning.

The tranquility after the hilarity,

Bid farewell to a stage of life,

I found heartwarming left behind after the hilarity,

Later, heartwarming disappeared. What was left after heartwarming disappeared?

The meaning of life is really a scary topic,

The more I live burningly, the more I feel that nothing is left, and the more terrifying the tranquility becomes.

Later I discovered: "Why am I looking for eternity?", The topic "The Meaning of Life" should not be "Heaven and Eternity". The "Meaning of Life" is "What do people live to do?"

I found that people have minds, just like blanks. People can think and create. The human minds will be hungry, people have to fill in the blanks with color.

I have made sure that life has meaning. People have something to do in life. People's minds will be hungry. People should think, enrich their minds, and fill in the blanks with color. The meaning of life is "diversity."

My goal is to tell the people I love:

"Life has meaning, you should cherish yourself."

But the answers of "the human heart will be hungry", "diversity" and "filling in the blanks with color" are too abstract.

So I wrote the book "The Consensus of Heart", which changed from "people's hearts will be hungry" to "people will be hungry".

I must eat, you must eat, people cannot refuse to eat, humans have the only choice, eat,Eat cherishedly,

Human beings have something to do when they are alive, and the meaning of life is to "eat together."

I answered the reason of "cherishing".

I explained the reason why I should manage you, and you should manage me.

I explained that "life has a common answer."

The author has answered the meaning of life, Hunger is the reason to move forward.

The author found "what humans should do in the future", "The direction of mankind", "Taiwan's direction", "certain things", "the purpose of education", "the reason for love", "the reason for goodness."

Section 5 : Taiwan's reaction.

The author's hometown is Taiwan. In order to counter Confucius, Taiwan searched for Taiwan's value, but could never find it.

The people of Taiwan have a deep affection for cows. Cows work hard and are not afraid of hardship, so the localists say that Taiwan's value is the spirit of the cow.

This is a strange thing, The new answer to counter Confucius is cow.

The localists paradoxically shout for the cow spirit, but at the same time they shout for "seeking Taiwan's values."

The President and the Minister of Education shout about Taiwan's value, but they cannot explain what Taiwan's value is.

And after I emailed my book to many professors, I wrote in the book: "

The meaning of life is diversity and eating together. "

President Tsai Ing-wen suddenly declares that Taiwan's values are "diversity and happy together ."

Did President Tsai Ing-wen discover the value of Taiwan? Why is this answer and what is the reason? What about the process of finding answers? What about old ideas being challenged?

Then the localists cheered happily that Taiwan has a direction and that Taiwan will move toward "diversity."

But is life really meaningful?"

My goal was blocked by Tsai Ing-wen.

When I try to tell Taiwanese people that "the meaning of life is diversity,"

There was a city councilor who initiated a referendum on the same-sex marriage laws. That councilor considered that the referendum was a show of support for the same-sex marriage laws.

But this is a strange thing. Are human rights determined by voting?

The city councilor joined several opinion leaders to promote the referendum.

And among those opinion leaders, there was a philosophy teacher.

What are the arguments for supporting same-sex marriage laws?

Are same-sex marriage laws related to "the meaning of life"?

The philosophy teacher Zhu's book became a popular book in that referendum. （ISBN：9789869278645）

In his book it is written,

Philosophy teacher Zhu doesn't believe that anyone can do three things:

1. Find the final answer to the meaning of life.

2. Prove that answer.

3. Forcing Teacher Zhu to accept it.

Teacher Zhu said: "Because there is no answer to the meaning of life, Taiwan should move towards diversity."

But "life has no answer" only infers that Taiwan should not necessarily move toward diversity.

"Teacher Zhu is an idiot" cannot deduce "Taiwan should move toward diversity."

Teacher Zhu plagiarized,

Teacher Zhu has no answer.

Teacher Zhu firmly believed that there was no answer, and suddenly he had the answer of "diversity".

Jue Chang, my goal is

"life is really meaningful".

But Teacher Zhu said that life is meaningless, same-sex marriage laws are meaningless, and no one can force others to accept that "same-sex marriage laws are meaningful."

Taiwan suddenly shouted "diversity",

But life still has no meaning,

My goal is still not achieved.

Section 6 : Real.

Jue Chang, my goal is

"Life is really meaningful, and you should cherish yourself."

Perhaps the teachers are also afraid of the topic of the meaning of life,

So I narrowed my goal,

Change from "Life is really meaningful, you should cherish yourself" to "This is true, you should cherish yourself."

The control group played racing games while awake.

The experimental group played a racing game while drunk.

This can prove that people should be sober.

The control group did not maintain the environment;

The experimental group maintains the environment,

This proves that people should care about their hometown.

The control group's broadcaster warned,

The experimental group's broadcaster said: "The king is great",

This proves the importance of supervision,

This proves that broadcasters should belong to the people,

I proved democracy.

The control group was a room without food,

The experimental group was a room with food.

This proves that people will be hungry.

The control group was an empty room,

The experimental group was a room with entertainment and mobile phones.

This can prove that people's minds will be hungry, People should think and enrich their minds.

I throw away the word "meaning of life",

My new goal is: "This is true. People have things to do in life. People should think, enrich their minds, and care about their hometown." This will still be true ten thousand years from now,

And I've proven it.

Dr. King said: "I have a dream."

 我的目標是：生命真的有意義

traditional values, universal values,

People debate the values.

Should Taiwanese people love Taiwan?

Can people be selfish?

Profit and justice conflict,

Morality is a lofty value, and democracy is a value.

The majority decides, listen to the words of the saints,

Who can point to a happy future?

Democracy is just a value.

Democratic values, Taiwan values, Universal values,

People kept shouting like this,

And when I share with others:

"Universal values are wrong,

Jue Chang, I prove that democracy is objective,"

All I hear is the sounds of broken hearts.

Section 7 : Conclusion.

Taiwan's President and Minister of Education have thrown away the cow spirit; Now they say: "Taiwan should move towards diversity." But the Minister of Education did not say "life is really meaningful."

Taiwan passed same-sex marriage laws. Are the same-sex marriage laws meaningful?

Are same-sex marriage laws right?

There is no standard answer to goodness;

Same-sex marriage laws aren't necessarily right, are they?

Taiwan shouts diversity,

Really? What's the proof method? Who proved it?

Jue Chang, my goal is "real",

Why is the Minister of Education advocating for diversity but not providing any proof?

Taiwan's president says democracy is a value; National Taiwan University did not correct it.

Jue Chang, my goal is "real",

Please say it out loud:

"Universal values are wrong,

Jue Chang proves that democracy is real."

　我的目標是：生命真的有意義

我的目標是：生命真的有意義
My Goal Is：Life Is Really Meaningful.
（中英雙語版）

作　　者／決長（Jue Chang）

出版者／美商 EHGBooks 微出版公司

發行者／美商漢世紀數位文化公司

臺灣學人出版網：http：//www.TaiwanFellowship.org

地　　址／106 臺北市大安區敦化南路 2 段 1 號 4 樓

電　　話／02-2701-6088 轉 616-617

印　　刷／漢世紀古騰堡®數位出版 POD 雲端科技

出版日期／2024 年 11 月

總經銷／Amazon.com

臺灣銷售網／三民網路書店：http：//www.sanmin.com.tw

　　　　　三民書局復北店

　　　　　地址／104 臺北市復興北路 386 號

　　　　　電話／02-2500-6600

　　　　　三民書局重南店

　　　　　地址／100 臺北市重慶南路一段 61 號

　　　　　電話／02-2361-7511

全省金石網路書店：http：//www.kingstone.com.tw

定　　價／新臺幣 450 元（美金 15 元／人民幣 100 元）

www.ingramcontent.com/pod-product-compliance
Lightning Source LLC
Chambersburg PA
CBHW012016050726
47590CB00009B/3205